This We Know

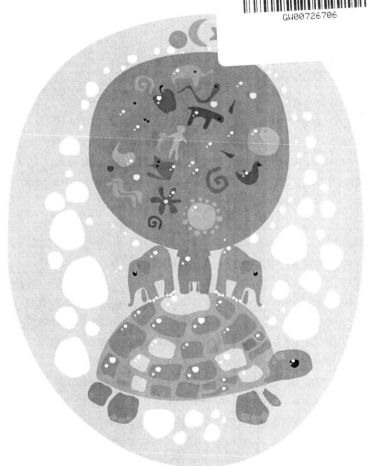

Tom Evans

This We Know

First Edition Published in Great Britain 2012

ISBN 978-1-849-14307-3

© Copyright Tom Evans

www.tomevans.co

The purpose of this book is to educate and entertain. The author and publisher of this book do not dispense medical or psychological advice. You should not use the techniques herein for treatment of any physical or medication issues without seeking the advice of a qualified medical practitioner. In the event you use any advice from this book, the author and publisher assume no responsibility for your actions.

To Louise, for giving me all the Space and Time in the world

This We Know

What ever befalls the Earth, befalls the Daughters and Sons of the Earth.

Times They Are Certainly a Changin'.

Humans did not weave the Rich Web of Life, they are merely a Strand on It.

All we need is Love and Money can't buy it for You.

All Things are Connected.

This We Know.

Inspired by Chief Seattle and other luminaries

Note to reader

None of this book is necessarily true.

Some of the facts may well be wrong.

It is important that you verify everything for yourself.

The author is human and making mistakes is part of the game.

Contents

One |
This We Know

Our Sun orbits the centre of our galaxy every 220,000 years. It has now completed about 25 orbits. We can think of these as cosmic years from the Sun's perspective. It probably has another 25 of its 'years' to go before it dies.

There are currently around 7 billion human mouths on Planet Earth that would like to be fed.

Humanity on this blue-green jewel of the cosmos represents just a small fraction of the living biomass.

Planet Earth houses an amazing, bizarre and bewildering array of other life forms. Some remain rooted to the earth. Some can fly. Many can swim. Some never see the light of day.

All can replicate and evolve as they do. All rely on each other in what is known as the Food Chain.

The 7 billion or so human mouths though are a little different. Their main difference is their ability to be self aware, to varying degrees. They also possess an appetite not just for food and an insatiable desire to ask questions.

Some questions that they ask remain unanswered.

Questions like "Why are we here?"

And "What's the point?"

The very asking of some of these questions have led to an incredible understanding of their place in the cosmos.

They know they revolve around a star they call the Sun. They believe the distance from their home star is perfect for life-as-they-know-it.

They believe they live in the Goldilocks Zone. Not too hot, not too cold.

They now know that their home star is one of hundreds of billion stars in their galaxy. They have recently found out that many other stars also have planets too. What's more, they know their galaxy is just one of a billion or more galaxies.

Despite knowing all of this, many of the 7 billion mouths feel incredibly alone.

This they know.

Two |
Right This Minute

The annual net human population
growth on the planet is over 70
million per year.

It will take an average reader about a minute to take in one of these purposely short 'chapters'. Perhaps it will take a little longer to ponder their significance.

So, as you read this, approximately 250 new human mouths will be born and require feeding. Around the same time, just over 100 human mouths will cease to move and will return from where ever they think they came from.

You will notice the difference between these two numbers. A little more digging reveals this disparity is greater in areas on the planet where there is less ability to feed these mouths.

Each new batch of 250 mouths are blissfully unaware of this. They don't even gain any degree of awareness of self for two to three years. By the time they get to age seven, most of them will realise that they are not necessarily the centre of the Universe.

At the other end of the age spectrum, many of those mouths who are checking out also lose their sense of self nowadays. Old age dementia is on the rise with the increase of life span. It has the beneficial side effect of taking the fear out of death.

It is perhaps somewhat ironic that some people check in and out of the planet with no hair, no teeth and an inability to feed themselves.

For many, the increased costs of caring for those that are living longer is wiping out money and assets amassed in their Living Years. This means, for many mouths, they come in with no money and leave with none too.

Things have a way of evening out over time. Nothing real can be destroyed and nothing unreal can persist.

Right at this minute, this is what's occurring.

Three | Dream Time

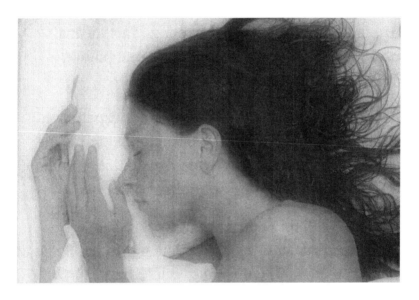

Randy Gardner holds the scientifically documented record for the longest period a human being has intentionally gone without sleep not using stimulants of any kind. In 1964, he stayed awake for 11 days.

While you are reading this and awake, about 2 billion people are asleep.

Quite a few are snoring. Some of them are insomniacs who want to fall asleep but can't seem to nod off.

Around half of them are dreaming. This means every minute of every day, around one billion dreams are playing out.

At the same time, 5 billion people are experiencing a form of waking dream. About one billion people are on the Internet at any one time. Another billion are watching TV. Some are doing both.

Around 3 billion people are at work. Some are dreaming of what it would be like not to be. Some of them are dreaming of what it would be like to be rich and happy. Some of them are dreaming up ways to have a better life for themselves and others.

About one billion people are dreaming of what it would be like to lose some weight. About one billion people are wondering where their next meal is coming from.

Of the 5 billion or so people who are awake, 3 billion or so live in cities polluted by light and airborne particulates.

This means that in those short magical hours between dusk and the other Dream Time, only a precious few people could actually look up and see the stars.

For some of them, the clouds in both senses, may not even part sufficiently for them to look.

So out of all these 7 billion souls sharing a journey on this blue-green jewel we call Earth, only a relative handful are even looking up at any time.

Attention is focussed in and down. Dreams nest inside dreams. Co-creation of our current reality is thus achieved.

As a result, for many, there is no Up-Side.

Four |
Spaceship Earth

It's estimated that our brains contain 80 billion neurons. This is about the same as the number of stars in a medium sized galaxy. This may not be a coincidence.

Our Home moves at about 66,000 miles an hour around its parent star. This means all the inhabitants travel about half a billion miles a year on their Spaceship Earth.

The Sun itself is moving around 500,000 miles an hour around the centre of the galaxy.

The Earth is just over 24,000 miles in circumference at the equator. It revolves on its axis in what 7 billion life forms refer to as being 24 hours. This means the ground under your feet is moving at over 1000 miles an hour, unless you are near one of the Poles.

We are in constant motion. Yet, for many, life stands still. For some it even goes backwards.

Spaceship Earth weighs in at around 5.972 sextillion tonnes. A sextillion is 1,000,000,000,000,000,000,000. That's a lot of noughts! A million billion indeed.

Of that, around 0.02% is water and 97.5% of the water is in the oceans. The air we breathe is just a millionth of the weight of the Earth.

All life forms on the planet weigh in at between 1000 to 2000 billion tonnes (there is some debate over the exact number). Of that humanity clocks in at 100 million tonnes.

Those one billion or so overweight people are doing their best to change these statistics. Those that are malnourished are balancing things out.

When we compare our weight to the air and water that keeps us alive, we are insignificant. We are almost weightless.

Our brains weigh in at around 2 to 3 kilograms. So if you add the weight of all our brains together, they are an even more minuscule amount of matter in the bigger scheme of things. Yet we take them so seriously.

Yet what makes our brain so remarkable though is that it seems to have gained the ability to be self aware and to ask questions about how it came to be.

Note in passing that all other brains for all other life forms are no less remarkable. Self awareness too is not restricted to humans. Species such as chimpanzees, magpies and dolphins can all recognise themselves in a mirror.

As we can see as children grow up, self awareness increases in waves and steps. Every seven years or so, a new version of Us arrives.

What we never know in one state is what the higher state of awareness will bring. We also do not know the upper limit of our capabilities.

Five |
What Do We Know?

The atomic clocks on the orbiting
GPS satellites run about 7.2
microseconds a day faster than
clocks on the ground.

You would be mistaken if you thought whoever wrote this book knows a lot of stuff.

In fact, the author just knows how to conjure up a set of linked questions, thoughts and memes that form a line of enquiry. His main skill is knowing how to wonder about something and how to look up the answer on the Internet.

The answers have been worked out by people who have asked similar questions and had the skill, tenacity and brain power to iterate towards something close to the right answer. The author did genuinely not know many of these facts until he started writing the book. He is taking it on trust, as might you, that they are true.

Truth is only a measure of how well what we observe fits our personal model of how things work.

We assemble our knowledge into models. We make predictions, and machines, based on these models. When observation deviates from prediction, or the machine breaks down, we refine these models. In this way, we get to 'know' more and more stuff.

For example, before the Space Age where we could actually look at our planet and confirm it was a globe, the non-Flat World model could only be inferred by observation.

At first, the horizon could be thought of as the edge of the world until brave souls circumnavigated it. When we started to go up in the air, at first with balloons and then aircraft, the curvature of the Earth was plain to see. The model fitted prediction.

A model of the world as a flat disc supported by an elephant standing on a tortoise is at the very least quite attractive. Not knowing what the tortoise is standing on is no less perplexing than some Big Answers yet to be known to some Big Questions.

The Flat Earth model has some usefulness. We think nothing of navigating across our round world with a flat map, for example. The screen of a GPS navigation system is also flat although, somewhat ironically, it is fed from data from an interconnected sphere of man-made orbiting 'moonlets'.

By asking the simple question, "What do we know?", with humility and in awe of the world we live in, we set new wheels in motion.

What if, for example, the elephant and tortoise represent, at a metaphorical level, unseen forces that make our reality 'real'?

We 'know' now much more than we used to know. The acquisition of knowledge is exponential and, if you think about it, linked to exponential population growth.

When more and more people know more and more 'things', we gain more and more knowledge.

Simples!!

Six |
What Don't We Know

The ancient Greeks had 12 main
Olympian gods and goddesses.
There were hundreds, if not
thousands, of demigods. Virtually
every object had a god or goddess
associated with it.

Despite amazing mastery over the physical world, we don't really know how we really got here.

What seems to happen is that the less people actually really know how we got here, the more vociferously they proclaim they do actually know the answer.

Take those of a religious persuasion for example. Out of the 7 billion people on the planet, around 5 and a half billion sort of believe there is a God who set the whole kit and caboodle in motion.

Out of those 5 and a half billion, there are followers of four main religions, and their many off shoots, who claim to know that their God is the only true God, and that the others are mere pretenders.

There are some slightly more enlightened and ecumenical souls who have twigged there is a good chance their gods are one and the same. Some 'know' though with such conviction that their's is the 'true path' that they will even kill others who disagree with their belief. This applies equally to all faiths up and down the Ages.

There are about one and a half billion people who don't follow these faiths. Out of this number, there are around half a billion Buddhists who see 'God in all'.

There are around one billion who don't believe in a Creator at all. Many of these atheists just don't give the idea of God a second thought. Many follow the 'God' of money, or Mammon.

Some lucky souls just get on with life, often living in a more holy and gracious manner than those who do 'believe'.

Some diehard atheists believe all can be explained by a new God of Science. Such is their self-belief that this is claimed to be knowledge. They know the entire Universe was created in a Big Bang, 14 or so billion years ago and there is no need for a Creator.

Armed with this knowledge, scientists even create their own mini-Suns in the form of hydrogen bombs. They create mini-Big Bangs in particle colliders. They are their own New Gods. Science is the New Dogma.

If there are two things we really do know they are these.

Firstly, once we think we know everything, we stop learning. Secondly, we 'know' exponentially more now than we used to know, therefore there is undoubtedly exponentially more still to know.

Seven |
Matters of Fact

$$\frac{x^3 - y^2}{\sqrt{z}} = 2\sqrt{\frac{(x^a - y^b)(3z + 2x - y^3)}{a^3 + b^2}}$$

$$\sqrt{\frac{a^x + \frac{1}{2}b^x}{y^2}} \cdot \frac{z^3}{a^3} = \frac{(a^2 + b^2 + x^2 + y^2)(x^3 - b^3)}{\sqrt{3x - 2y^3 - z^3}}$$

$$\sqrt[3]{\frac{(2xy)^2 \cdot (3ab + 3x)^3}{x^3 y^2}} = \frac{5x^2 + 3y^3 - a^3 - b^3}{z^2 a^2 b^2}$$

Over 250 million Tweets are posted
each day on Twitter. One in every
thirteen people on Earth is on
Facebook. People spend over 700
billion Earth minutes per month on
the site.

When it comes to discovering facts, humans are masters at it.

We know with some accuracy that the speed of light is 299,792,458 metres per second. Note though that is not true in all circumstances across the whole Universe - and all time.

You only have to go 93 million miles from our planet, into the centre of the Sun, where light speed slows down to a snail's pace. It's thought light generated inside the Sun takes anything from 10,000 to 100,000 years to reach the surface.

Even on Earth itself, light in the water in your own bath tub slows down by 1.333 times from its speed in the vacuum of space.

Perhaps unlike any other species on the planet, we are equipped not only with this ability to discover facts. We also the possess the ability to change them.

We take it as fact that there are 7 billion people on the planet and that, by 2050, this will rise to 9 billion or more.

The jury is still out on this but imagine if we all agreed that it was a 'fact' that this growth was unsustainable.

We could all agree that 7 billion people were quite enough and we should do something about balancing birth and death rates.

All it would take is world leaders to convene and agree to start education programmes in their countries. The Catholic Church would have to change its ludicrous doctrine on the non-use of condoms. Members of the Twitterati and the huge 'virtual country' which is Facebook would start tweeting and poking their thoughts on the matter. The message would circle the globe at something approaching the speed of light.

Some would do their bit to control their breeding voluntarily. Others would need to be educated, incentivised or cajoled. It is a fact that one billion Chinese have already had a go at this.

This would not limit life for humans on Earth but help sustain the species. Every 100 years or so there would be 7 billion New People experiencing life on this wonderful planet.

Never before in history have we been in a better position to come to global consensus on matters of fact that affect us all.

Now, of course, it could well be that the planet can support 70 billion people or more.

For this to be viable, we would simply have to learn some new facts about how to do this without upsetting the rest of the interconnected biosphere.

Note too that recently some scientists may have discovered things that go faster than light. Other scientists have then challenged these reports. Just possibly, all that is going on is for opinion to sway and the results then follow the collective thought pattern.

This we just don't know - yet!

Eight |
In a Nutshell

Coconuts aren't nuts. They are
drupes (from the Greek dryppa,
meaning "tree-ripened"). Drupes
are fruit with a fleshy outer coating
enclosing a hard shell containing a
seed.

No matter how many facts we collect, in a nutshell, all that we can ever really know is a model that works for us that allows us to get by in life.

We think we know for certain that we will die at some point and cease to exist. Some of course 'know' they will survive after their death. Some of those 'know' they will go to Heaven, or some to Hell. Others 'know' they will come back and live a near infinite set of existences, perhaps until they reach some form of Nirvana.

Others 'know' that this life is all they have got. As a result, a choice of paths exists. They could choose a hedonistic, selfish lifestyle. Alternatively, they could treasure every moment of every day, seeing beauty and awe in all around. A mix of these two paths is also a possibility.

A new level of knowing again can be attained when we simply know it is OK for each of us to hold our own model of the world.

It is a Good Thing that we know different things and hold different beliefs.

Conversely it is a Bad Thing to attempt to enforce our own model on others based on what we think we know.

This is the way the Universal Mind Pool increases and we end up knowing more 'stuff'. The alternative route leads to oppression and a return to a Darker Age. Conversely, just knowing this is a possibility leads to a Bright Future indeed.

Let's recap on what we think we know.

There are 7 billion of us hurtling through space at an incredible speed. One billion of us overweight and one billion are malnourished. We represent a small fraction of all life forms on the planet. Our planet revolves around one of billions of stars in one of billions of galaxies, in the Known Universe.

Incidentally, for all we know, this Universe is just one of countless Multiverses.

The weird part is this. We possess a tiny amount of matter we call a brain which is aware of itself and its relative position in the scheme of things. We just don't quite know how we got here.

Some scientists theorise that two generations of stars had to explode in order to generate the heavy atoms to form our planet - and Us. This makes us sentient stardust.

Over five billion of us proclaim to 'know' though that some god or other created everything and Us.

Perhaps this was just by way of setting off a Big Bang as an experiment to see what happened.

Perhaps an infinity of Big Bangs have been set off by a Creator who was bored and wanted to brighten up a dull day. Not that days existed before Time too was created of course.

Perhaps, as some think or claim to know, we are all aspects of that very Creator. Perhaps we created ourselves so we could look back at ourselves and say, "Wow, that was one neat trick you pulled off there!"

So armed with this conjecture, as it is not knowledge yet at least, we could embark on a new phase in our journey on Spaceship Earth.

Except for a few lucky astronauts, we are all stuck here for this lifetime at least. So why not see if all 7 billion of us can get along better and make the best of what we have and the most of our time on this special planet?

Nine | Sisters and Brothers in Arms

The average life of a dollar bill is just
18 months.

Before you read these next chapters, you should know a few things.

The author doesn't claim to know the answers or to have any agenda. He doesn't know for certain if God exists or we are some freak accident of nature.

He does think though we are at an amazing point in our history and on the brink of a new level of 'knowing'.

He doesn't necessarily know how to go about implementing what follows but he has heard about the 100th Monkey Syndrome.

Apparently when enough monkeys (or people) on an isolated island learn a new skill, monkeys (or people) on neighbouring islands pick up that skill by some sort of psychic osmosis. If true and not simply apocryphal, all that is needed for change is that enough people start to think and act differently.

Note in passing that these 'islands' could even be planets spread across multiple star systems across multiple galaxies.

This means a small change in thought pattern of one small insignificant brain from one of 7 billion people can instigate a change across Space and Time. Each of us is potentially capable of igniting such sparks.

In past times we have looked for leadership from religious leaders, politicians and latterly scientists.

We know that politicians don't really know how to run a country, they are all 'having a go' and largely experimenting.

We know even religious leaders don't know for sure that God exists.

We know scientists don't know for sure how we got here.

We know things aren't right and could be better. Yet, any change of any significance will not come from those who purport to lead us, it can only come from each one of us.

For example, the annual military spend globally is over 1 trillion dollars.

Just imagine if that money was spent not keeping the peace but creating the peace. Just imagine if that money was spent feeding the malnourished and educating the obese. Just imagine if that money was spent on healthcare or research into ecological power generation.

We can all imagine better ways to spend that money. We could just divvy it up 7 billion ways so it would get spent back into the economy.

Or why not blow it all on a global party every year to celebrate we are all alive on the same lump of rock?

Is this stance naive? Just imagine if it wasn't and that within 100 years it could come to pass.

Pass it on!!!

Ten |
Changing Tides

Even with current technology, wave power could provide one fifth of our energy needs.

While it might be thought it's not possible to redirect the global annual military expenditure constructively, it is something we can at least imagine.

Indeed many military initiatives are currently labelled as peace keeping forces. Many personnel from the armed forces are used to help with national disasters. So things have changed already in just the last 100 years as our awareness and knowledge of global affairs has increased.

We know more now about how things are connected on many levels. Economics, weather patterns and even plate tectonics all have seasonality and all exhibit occasional chaotic behaviour which is seemingly out of our control. They are of course often interlinked as an economic driver is often behind a military intervention or global rescue mission.

A tsunami on one part of the globe will be reported in seconds elsewhere. There will be a wave of chatter on the social networks within minutes that actually dwarves the size of the wave that created it, in terms of the numbers it touches. Cash, aid and resources will flood from people on one side of the planet over to people elsewhere that they have never met.

We act not out of pity but knowing what we have done is a Good Thing and that others will reciprocate if the situation was reversed and if they were able.

While the Western economies have benefited from resources from the Third World, the tide is turning.

Old bastions, old economic models and old dictatorships are crumbling as they are ultimately unsustainable. As mentioned, nothing unreal can persist.

Just go back one hundred years and we had no colour TV, no mobile phones and no space probes beaming back images from other worlds. These would be seen as magic. They were though thought about in the minds of novelists like Jules Verne and H.G. Wells.

Imagine then that it is simply our imagination that is driving everything all this time. This means as soon as we think we 'know' the world, the world as we know it changes as someone somewhere has had a bright idea.

What's more this applies at microscopic and universal levels. Quantum physicists might not be so much discovering new particles as imagining them into existence. Astronomers might not be detecting new planets but causing them to come into being.

God might not have lit the Blue Touch paper and sat back to see what happened. She may still be active today using each of us as agents.

Just imagine that these secrets have been known for years but the implications and ramifications of their use are so far reaching that they could be dangerous in the wrong hands.

Just imagine.

Eleven |
Wide Awake

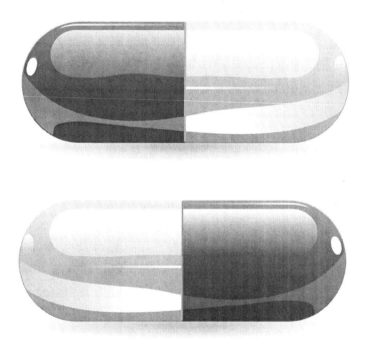

Americans consume 80 percent of
the world's supply of painkillers
which weighs in at more than 110 tons
of addictive opiates taken every
year.

When you are one of the 2 billion people sleeping and dreaming, you are not aware of the 5 billion people that are awake.

Conversely when we are awake, we don't give too much thought to all those people lost in their slumber and reverie.

Just imagine though if all the people who thought they were actually awake were really asleep but didn't know it. Now this is not so much like a film like The Matrix where we are purposely trapped and used for some nefarious purpose. Think about it more like that there are levels of awake-ness, like rungs of a ladder, that we are able to scale. Our current level of awake-ness is quite high but there may be other rungs yet to climb.

Now bearing in mind what we imagine has the tendency to come to pass, we can even have an influence on these heightened awakened states by taking flights of fancy.

So let's take another slightly ludicrous expenditure to task. The global annual sales for the pharmaceutical industry is perhaps also coincidentally somewhere around 1 trillion dollars.

The industry has undoubtedly had a direct impact on extending life expectancy and, in turn, the increase in the global population.

As such, it has had a beneficial hand in allowing 7 billion people to share a journey at the same time on Spaceship Earth. Some amazing research is going on to produce more targeted 'wonder drugs'. This is a Good Thing.

At the same time, over consumption and reliance on pills has resulted in many people being addicted to some types of drugs and often then needing other drugs to counteract their side effects.

Just imagine though that, as for the military spend, most of the need for drugs in the first place wasn't necessary. The money could then be used to improve factors that fundamentally affect health care like infrastructure, education and sanitation. It's perhaps just that the people making money out of making drugs don't yet know how to make money in other ways.

The people who use the drugs are as responsible as the drug companies in consenting to this way of being. By taking a pill, we hope problems will go away. By not taking a pill, the problem can also go away.

For example, carrying extra weight on our skeleton is one of the primary causes of back pain. So rather than eating less, exercising and dieting, some people end up taking both weight loss pills and painkillers.

Just imagine an even wilder dream. Imagine, if by entering an even more awake state, you did not readily succumb to illness or dis-ease in the first place.

Or imagine that your hands, and everyone else's hands, could channel healing energy to reduce the need for drugs at all.

Just imagine if this energy is available on tap for all of us ... and it was free. What would happen as a result?

Just imagine.

Twelve |
Bending Time

The Amondawa tribe in the Amazon have no word for time. They have no names for a week, a month or a year. Domesticated dogs are the same. They just know when it's 'walk-time' and 'food-time'.
A 'day' for an astronaut orbiting the Earth lasts about 90 minutes.

One of the major benefits of the clock of time is that it stops everything from happening all at once.

The thought experiment where you could go back and kill your own grandfather can only lead to grief. As people around us largely stick around, we can only assume this paradox isn't playing out that often. There are however some missing persons whose absence never quite gets fully explained.

In the same way our self-awareness creates and modulates the space in which we inhabit, it is well known our sense of time is affected by our consciousness.

If your appointment with a doctor is delayed and you have read all the magazines in the waiting room, those minutes stretch into hours. Those busy weekends with friends seem to end all too soon. Those with unwelcome family might stretch out interminably.

Times spent 'in the zone' have a magical quality where time seems to stretch out to fit the task at hand.

Time is only as fixed as we think it is.

People make the excuse of there not being enough hours in the day.

The implication of there being as many hours as you need though mean there is nowhere to hide and no excuses.

You will have heard the phrase, "If you want something done, give it to a busy person."

The reason this works is that when we are busy our sense of time alters and we don't just get more done, we 'create' the time for it to get done.

What's more, while we 'know' this is true, our science will tell us it is an illusion or trick of the mind. The reason for this is because we are blessed with two minds.

One mind we commonly refer to as our left brain sits inside space and time. The other that we call our right brain sits everywhere and 'everywhen' else.

This is the gift that allows us to inhabit space and time whilst simultaneously creating the space and time in which we live.

Note too that the Ancient Greeks knew a few things that have only recently been re-discovered. They had two gods, Kronos and Kairos. Kronos looked after space and time while Kairos managed the heavens. They also knew our minds had the ability to connect with either god.

This they knew.

Thirteen |
Bending Space

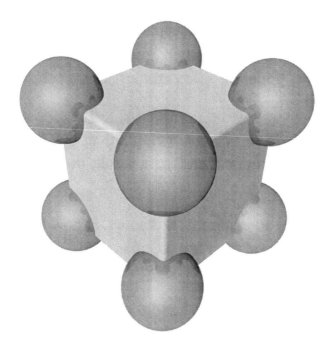

The speed of our breath affects the perceived passage of time – and our longevity. Ask any elephant or tortoise. Note that even the Earth 'breathes' as the Moon rotates around it.

Thanks to luminaries like Newton and Einstein, we have become Masters of Space.

We can send a space probe to another planet and have it arrive within seconds of planned time, within metres of its planned landing point.

This is an amazing achievement for sentient stardust. It is worth though knowing why great scientists, philanthropists and artists are referred to as luminaries.

Now there is an obvious metaphorical link between being 'en-light-ened' and, as a result, then being 'en-lighten-ing'.

What is not so explored, or known, is how thought, light, space and time are so entangled.

Through Newton's in-spired Laws of Gravity and Einstein's illuminated Theories of Relativity, we have an amazing degree of understanding of how matter and light interact.

Note that Newton's ideas are referred to as Laws but Einstein's Theories could be thought of as more like a work-in-progress.

This is how we now know when the sun will set and rise to seconds of accuracy.

We can predict Venus transits, eclipses of the Sun and the exact hour of a high tide on any place on the planet many centuries into the future.

In this mechanistic Universe, we adopt the role of both observer and time keeper. It runs like clockwork where someone else wound it up and set it ticking.

What place is there in this model of the world for the concept of Free Will? Is everything that plays out on Spaceship Earth a mere bagatelle or sub-plot?

Real rocket scientists use the gravitational pull of planets to slingshot space probes into new trajectories at even faster speeds. For how this works, imagine hitting a golf ball at 50 miles an hour at the front of an express train travelling at 100 miles an hour. If it hit it straight on, it would rebound at about 150 miles an hour or so.

So, as far as planetary dynamics are concerned, there is perhaps the idea of a 'free lunch'.

When the Earth itself, with it's 7 billion awarenesses, has been used for such slingshots, the probes have been measured to be just off from their projected timings by a few milliseconds. Nobody knows quite why, even taking Einstein's relativity into account.

Could it be then that we don't quite 'know' what effect consciousness and awareness have when they interact with space and time? Perhaps noticing such phenomena are a nudge for us to find out.

Note too that the author does not know if this latter conjecture is true or not. He does know however by exploring whether it might be, or not, will lead to new knowings.

This he knows.

Fourteen |
The Tipping Point

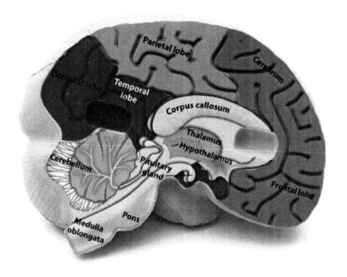

It is thought that the main function
of the corpus callosum, the butterfly
shaped structure that connects our
left and right brains, is to inhibit one
side of the brain so the other can
operate. It does this without us
giving it a second thought.
Amazing things happen when we
inhibit its inhibiting action.

Our left and right brains do more than sit 'in time' and 'out of time'. They also mediate between what is known and what is unknown.

It's an urban myth that the left brain is logical and the right brain is creative. Areas in both sides of the brain are active, and interactive, in logical and creative processes.

Where any asymmetry can be shown to exist, it is that areas of the left brain tend to operate on learned processes while the right brain tends to take on board the acquisition of new skills.

So a better model might be that the left brain generates thought and our experience of what we call reality. At the same time, our right brain receives new thought and experiences and passes them to the left to make sense of them.

Note too that this is just a model. As the brain is neurologically plastic and re-wirable, all we need to do to alter even this model is to think it might not be true.

Note that any full model of consciousness will have to take on board other mind centres inside and outside our bodies.

Such ramblings in themselves are indeed aimed at scrambling old paradigms and encouraging new thought.

54

By doing so, the old ways in which we think about ourselves and our interaction with the world get turned on their heads.

We can allow ourselves a certain luxury and indulgence.

What if the world was not a cold, unloving place where we are all isolated individuals destined to be born, live and die? What if it was a playground designed, by us and for us, for us to experience, evolve and grow?

What if the so called Laws of the Universe are not fixed in stone for all time? What if they are phenomena for us to observe and interact with and change?

So, in an instant, we can train our brains to act and react differently from before and this will have a direct effect on the space we inhabit. When we do this collectively, the effects are amplified accordingly.

Such a revelation can only augur the arrival of a new level of knowing and a new level of understanding.

The mere thought that this is even a remote possibility brings us to a Tipping Point in our evolution.

Fifteen |
Crossing the Chasm

The longest single span bridge in the world is currently the Akashi-Kaikyō Bridge in Japan, with a main span of 6532 feet.

A wise person once said, "Do not cross a chasm in two leaps."

If we are to get to know a new way of being, it would be naive to get all 7 billion people to agree to adopt it all at once on midnight GMT on New Year's Eve. Two billion of us may be asleep after all.

People will still start arguments. When fists come out they will break into fights. When guns and knifes come out, they will break into wars. The World's Policemen will keep fighter planes, gunships and missiles until all 7 billion people stop arguing and start to really enjoy living on this special planet.

Drugs companies will still make drugs as long as people want to take them. Dis-ease will still arise when minds and bodies are unsettled. Accidents will happen too. Popping a pill or three is like taking a Magic Bullet of a different kind. It is no bad thing if it is a means to an end, not a dependency.

So if we are faced with the current Way of Things and want to cross the chasm to a new paradigm, it's best not to throw the baby out with the bath water.

This transition is a journey not a revolution. New knowledge is to be gained from making the trip itself.

By building a bridge between the two states of being, people can simply cross when they feel good and ready.

They can also go across for a day trip or longer vacation to see what it's like. Then they could either stay or go back. If they do go back to check their Old Ways, they might bring more people back with them next time.

Crossing the bridge requires passing through a Toll Gate. And here's the thing. Nobody is taking any toll money; the toll is completely free. The only investment required is the acceptance to be open to a new way of knowing, being and doing.

What's more, it's not even mandatory to cross the chasm using the bridge. There are still two alternative paths open to everyone. It's just that crossing by the bridge is the simplest and easiest way.

Before explaining more about how to pass easily and simply through the Toll Gate, let's explore the other two paths so any decision can be made with 20:20 fore-sight.

Sixteen |
The Two Paths

Steve Fossett completed longest balloon flight aboard the Spirit of Freedom. The epic journey lasted 14 days 19 hours and 51 minutes and covered 20,602 miles. He was the first person to circumnavigate the earth solo in a balloon.

When faced with the challenge of crossing a deep ravine, building a bridge as a way to cross it is no mean feat of civil engineering.

It takes years of planning and a considerable amount of hard graft. Once the bridge is in place though, so many people benefit from it that we wonder how we ever managed without it. We get grumpy if it is taken out of service.

Before the bridge was in place, people only had two options. Either they could clamber down one steep side and scramble up the other. This route is tough and might be treacherous. There is often a gushing torrent of water at the bottom to cross that eroded the ravine over time.

The other route is entirely more graceful, although it could harbour other perils. One could use a hot air balloon to rise up and simply float across the ravine. The only dangers would be if you got blown off course or had a hard landing.

These two routes are of course metaphors.

Some people gain new knowledge and wisdom by descending into dark chasms. Others grow stronger and braver as a result of this type of journey. Some write their life story of their trials and tribulations to share with others so they do not have to experience the same fate.

In extreme cases, some even experience 'near-death' and return with seemingly super-sensible powers. Some never come back.

For those that take the lofty route, they simply live an ascetic life full of meditative practice and sometimes abstinence. There is nothing wrong with this route of course, excepting that the deep intricacies of the ravine, up close and personal, will never be experienced.

Where people make errors with either route is to attempt to preach to others that their path is the Right One.

One thing that we certainly know is this. Each of the 7 billion souls on the planet is free to choose their own way. By doing so the Universal Knowledge Pool deepens and widens.

"Beware those who claim to know The Way. There are many Paths of Return."

Seventeen |
Crossing the Bridge

The most expensive toll road in the world is the Nürburgring Nordschleife in Germany made famous by 24-hour races and its 154 turns. Performance cars, motorcycles, minivans and buses all jockey for space on the circuit. A trip around the 20.8 kilometers circuit will cost 26 euros.

Whether you are an individual, a family or any sized group, crossing the bridge over the ravine is easy - and free.

All you have to do is to decide to leave a harder way of life behind and to begin a new one. There is no need to follow a new religion or dump your old one - apart from one caveat.

If aspects of your old creed are fear-based or guilt-based, you should encourage its practitioners to re-examine that aspect of their faith. Change from the inside out is so much more effective.

A classic example is the Original Sin used by some branches of Catholicism. Humankind has not been cast out of heaven in order to do some sort of penance on an imperfect Earth by redeeming their sins. This is Dark Age, medieval thinking designed for purposes of control. Like all life forms, we can be better described as sophisticated, spiritual beings having an incarnate experience on one of the most sought after planets in the cosmos.

Fear-based practices from marketeers, governments, health care providers, insurance companies and financial institutions similarly will find it difficult on the other side. Their customer bases will simply not exist when they get to know a different way to be.

The Toll Gate you see is a magical force field. Without fear, guilt, sadness or anger, you can walk through it easily. Harbour any of these thoughts and you cannot get to the other side.

Before passing through it, you will pass several chutes that allow you to dump any such feelings into the ravine below. They fall into the torrential river and are taken out to sea for re-cycling.

You can let go of all fears knowing their only purpose was to protect you. On the other side of the bridge, there is nothing to fear as nothing is out to get you.

All guilt is no longer necessary. You are forgiven for any past transgressions. Their purpose was merely for you to learn and to know more as a result.

Any sadness you feel in your heart has no place on the other side. All those lost souls and opportunities will resolve and make sense in Good Time.

You can take any anger and dump it with thanks and love to those who have angered you. Their actions, no matter how wrong at the time, only served to educate and teach you something. They too were only learning.

For good measure, vent your anger by shouting into the wind.

Let it be heard by those souls still taking the treacherous trip down the ravine and to those lofty beings floating above in their balloons in the clouds.

After all, what do they really know that you don't?

Eighteen |
The Other Side

The normal human mind is only
capable of experiencing one
thought at a time. Think about what
you are thinking about right now
and that thought gets replaced by
the thought you are now having. Ask
any shaman and you will find this is
not a given.

When you are on the Other Side of the bridge, you find that life takes on a new quality. A magical world opens up for you where there is just enough time and infinite space.

Everything happens just when it needs to. You seem to be able to bend time and space around you. Frustrations vapourise as luck and good fortune become daily visitors. You find you can get loads done in what seems like no time at all. You soon forget what it was like to struggle.

On the other side, you may find some residual fears and doubts surface from time to time. See them as just tests to check you have really moved on. As you are having a good time too, the odd spot of guilt might raise its head too. Let it pass.

You discover that you can go back across the bridge with ease and mix with others yet to discover this new way of being. Being a good hearted person, you of course want to share your secret.

Here's where a new level of knowing should be brought to bear. It is up to everyone to chose their time to cross. Be careful not to evangelise in order to avoid being perceived in the same light as other fear-based creeds.

There is only one way to proceed. Show the way by example.

When people spot your change in fortune, they might also notice your change in complexion too. Only when they spot you are lucky in love and life is it time to point them at the bridge.

Those taking the other paths might even prick up their ears. There is no particular need any more for an ascension over the bridge. Heaven was and is already on Earth, not in the clouds. It took aeons to create this planet, and all the other Spaceships with living biospheres orbiting their own Suns. They are all versions of heaven.

There is no need either to drop into the ravine into some sort of personal Armageddon. There is an easier way.

Of course there will be those who question what you know. This is to be encouraged.

When you get to the other side of that first ravine, you find that there is a near infinite set of ravines yet to cross.

And here's the thing. Each time you cross one, you get to know even more still.

What's more, there are some mountains to scale too. From the top of such peaks amazing new vistas await.

This We Know.

Postscript 2112 | The Future's Bright

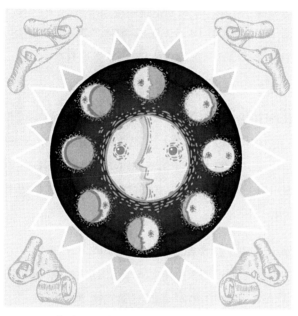

Out of the 7 billion people who were sharing their journey on Spaceship Earth back in 2012, there are only about 10 million of them who are still alive. Most of those who are still around were all under the age of ten when the book was first published. The rest of them, including the author, are all dead.

It's now the year 2112 and 100 years since the first edition of this book was published.

These days the new crop of human beings know quite a considerable number of new things that would appear to be like magic to people living back then. The 10 billion or so humans now sharing their ride on the Spaceship have really got their act together too.

That faster-than-light technology is now doing more than just providing all the Earth's transport and energy needs, with no reliance on fossil fuels. It being free has lead to transformation in the world's economies.

People love their Levitons, the wheel-less transporters that glide silently a foot or so off the ground. Their intelligent kinesthetic sensors, connected to The Grid, mean nothing ever bashes into anything else. There are no accidents. They do have artificial noise generators, with proximity detectors, to let people know they are coming though.

On the inter-city highways, or when you go across the ocean on a Tubeway, you just dial in where you are going and when you would like to get there. You can even doze off if you don't want to take in the view.

74

Off road the Levitons are great fun too, especially the single seaters. They can be joined together in convoys, both horizontally and vertically. Some amazing constructions can be seen on highways and byways.

The Lighter-Than-Airships have taken over the role that used to be performed by ocean going cruise liners. A trip on one of those is one amazing party in the sky. Some people stay up for years, circumnavigating the globe.

Back on terra firma, everyone can now afford to eat as much as they want and to keep themselves warm - or cool. Those that create and produce surpluses can trade freely and generate as much wealth as they need to acquire more chattels. Not many do as they have all they can possibly need. Most people choose to freely share with others their art and what used to be referred to as intellectual property.

People don't so much work any more but contribute and create, loving what they do.

What used to be thought of as a job, we now think of as being a calling. Many people take on two or more roles concurrently in a dynamically changing and enriching portfolio career.

The average life span of 120 years mean many people experience so much more of life than before.

The notion of retirement simply does not feature in our lives any more.

Elders tend to teach and advise and document their learnings though. Nobody has a pension these days as they are irrelevant. Sabbaticals every ten years or so aren't mandatory but everyone seems to take them to celebrate 10 more orbits of the Sun.

Incidences of cancer and old age dementia are rare. They are always studied in detail in order to know more about the seed thought patterns or mutations that caused them.

The political landscape varies little from country to country. It's become convention that parties don't use capital letters any more and they've all adopted the use of trendy hyphens. As a result, Conservatives have become conserve-atists and Communists call themselves commune-ists.

Most political and social systems could be best described as being like a liberal, humanistic, collective hedonism.

Everyone just seems to be having a Good Time these days. Nobody minds or begrudges doing their three years of National Public Service. Some volunteer for more.

Off planet, things are getting very interesting too.

The feasibility project to terraform the Valles Marineris - the Grand Canyon of Mars - is complete. The first Taikonauts are due to set foot on another planet in under a year's time.

The lead Taikonaut has her first words ready. She plans to say, "That's one small step for a woman ..."

The three interstellar micro-space probes have been beaming pictures back for 12 years from Epsilon Eridani, our nearest neighbouring Solar System.

At only 12 light years away, the trip only took 8 years to complete using the new faster-than-light drives. Their images arrive back at Earth almost instantaneously.

The probes arrival had been timed for the 1st of January 2100, to celebrate the most amazing 100 years humankind had ever experienced. They have yet to detect any signs of life-as-we-know-it. Other missions will be arriving at more distant systems in the next decade though.

On that same day, at the start of this new century, the Thirteen Moon calendar was finally adopted as standard Earth-wide.

Everyone now celebrates the same Day Out of Time on what used to be called the 25th July.

The twenty-first century had seen us pulling things back from the brink.

Now the ice caps have been fully restored, the sea-life in the oceans is fully back to pre-Industrial Revolution levels. That was a close call as so many species were close to extinction.

The freak weather patterns of the Twenties and Thirties had all but abated by the Seventies. Most of the low lying lands that had been inundated by flood water had now been reclaimed.

Pope Joan had done the most fabulous job harmonising all the world's religions. The full pantheon of 'gods' and 'goddesses' had become accepted and revered once again.

Mother Earth was once again recognised as the consciousness of Lady Gaia, orbiting the Sun God along with her travelling companion Sister Moon.

It was pretty much agreed that the one Creator of everything wasn't after all a 'He' or a 'She', more like an 'It'. Their omnipotence and omnipresence was a natural byproduct of being 'in' Every-Thing.

Pope Joan was also instrumental in bringing in the practice, in most countries, whereby politicians maintained a 51% female and 49% male ratio.

It became custom and practice for a female leader of a country to alternate terms with a male. Natural balance had become the order of the day.

The world's media had changed its approach completely. They reported on Good News, new learnings and acts of fruitful endeavour. Any Bad News was rare anyway and, if it did occur, was dealt with in documentaries analysing its source.

Great changes had transpired too in the global economy.

Forex traders were made redundant in the Fifties, when the single world currency came into being. Bankers became trusted servants of the people for the first time since their role had been created.

The armies and soldiers of the world became recognised as true heroes when they pitched up to help out in a crisis, with their amazing resources and know-how. Not many of them carried weapons, just tools.

Even the USA finally banned the possession of personal firearms, for anything but pure sport, as a concession to world peace in 2099.

Museums kept some as a reminder of course for generations to follow.

The healing arts had become fully understood and integrated with what used to be known as conventional healthcare. Most people knew someone in their family or village who could sort many ailments out. Hardly anyone ever took a pill.

By the end of the last century, no more people were born each year than died. Most of those who died chose the exact time and manner of their departure.

Living 'wakes' were all the rage. These celebrations of life brought all their friends and family together from all points of the globe.

It was just as well we could park our Levitons on top of each other. This was one of their neatest features. You could, of course, extract your Leviton at any time and all the others would just smoothly come together, filling the space left behind. It was equally useful they could drive us all home automatically and safely after we had a few drinks.

During the wake, the departing soul would distribute the assets they had amassed to their family and friends. The wake was then the last item of their expenditure.

Everyone left the planet owning absolutely nothing which was exactly how they arrived. Everything was in perfect karmic balance.

Accordingly, some parties went on for days and weeks, with the passing of the person being the final culmination of the lavish festivities.

At the end of the party, orbital cremations were becoming very popular too.

When you were ready to shed your mortal coil, you were sent into low Earth orbit in a levitating capsule. You could take as long as you like to look at the planet, for the last time.

When you were ready, you pressed the button for re-entry. Many people used the automatic setting that meant they would burn up as a bright shooting star right above the heads of their party guests.

This we could know - or something like it.

Tomography

Tom Evans first crossed his big ravine when he wrote his first book.

Beforehand he was an ex-BBC trained broadcast engineer who'd found himself in his mid-forties being a bored IT consultant. It all changed when, kind of by accident, he wrote a trilogy of interlocking, poetic life stories called 100 Years of Ermintrude. He then found that unwittingly he had stepped through the Toll Gate.

He found his fears about being ridiculed and his self doubt were completely unfounded. People seemed to like what he wrote. Glowing reviews flooded in. What's more, a new and completely unplanned career as an author's mentor came out of nowhere. He has since lost count of the people he has helped cross their ravine to change from being unpublished to being published authors.

His next two books explored the nature of creativity, and what blocks it. As a result of writing Blocks, he became known as a specialist at clearing writer's block. His next book The Art and Science of Light Bulb Moments even earned him the moniker of the Wizard of Light Bulb Moments.

What came next though involved him crossing yet another ravine. After writing his next non-fiction books, Flavours of Thought and Planes of Being, he crossed another bridge from being a writer's coach to being a healer, karmic mentor and modern day alchemist. His mission became clearer to him - to take the esoteric and make it exoteric - to make the un-known and un-understood into the known and understood.

As a result another bridge was crossed without him hardly even noticing. He has found himself opening a portal called Recipes for Fresh Thinking, which is possibly the world's first De-mystery School. It is a portal in two senses.

Its programmes such as Bending Time, The Cube of Karma, The Tree of Thought and Bending Space are designed to awaken the Inner Magician in everyone.

Together they have been described as being like a Software Upgrade for the Soul.

Tom knows for certain there are many more bridges yet to cross.

Also by Tom Evans

Fiction and Poetry

Soulwave

100 Years of Ermintrude

Non-fiction

Blocks | The Enlightened Way to Cure
Writer's Block

The Art and Science of Light Bulb Moments

Flavours of Thought

Planes of Being

Find out more at www.tomevans.co

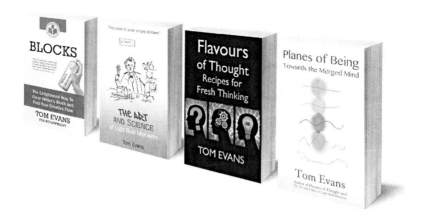

Connect with Tom

You can find Tom on Twitter, Facebook and
LinkedIn

www.facebook.com/thebookwright

www.twitter.com/thebookwright

www.linkedin.com/in/thebookwright

recipesforfreshthinking
CHANGE YOUR THOUGHTS, CHANGE YOUR MIND, CHANGE YOUR WORLD

For details of the Recipes for Fresh Thinking De-
Mystery School, visit

www.recipesforfreshthinking.com

bendingtime
CHANGE YOUR MIND | CHANGE YOUR TIME

To find out how to Bend Time, visit

www.bendingtime.info

Acknowledgements

This book was inspired 'un-knowingly' by my life partner while she was slumbering on the sofa one evening. She made me think about everyone else who was also 'asleep' at that time. Eternal thanks, as always, my Humangel Louise.

The book was further fuelled by a Soul Verse reading I had received earlier that same day from Sue Warwick. The Secret Man is now stepping out from the shadows.

The inspiration for the title, and meme, was provided by the haunting opening minute of the One World, One Voice album by Kevin Godley and Lol Creme.

For sanity checking and attention to detail, big thanks to Jackie Walker, who is always my Reader #001.

Image Credits

Lightning Source UK Ltd.
Milton Keynes UK
UKOW030630120713

213649UK00009B/199/P